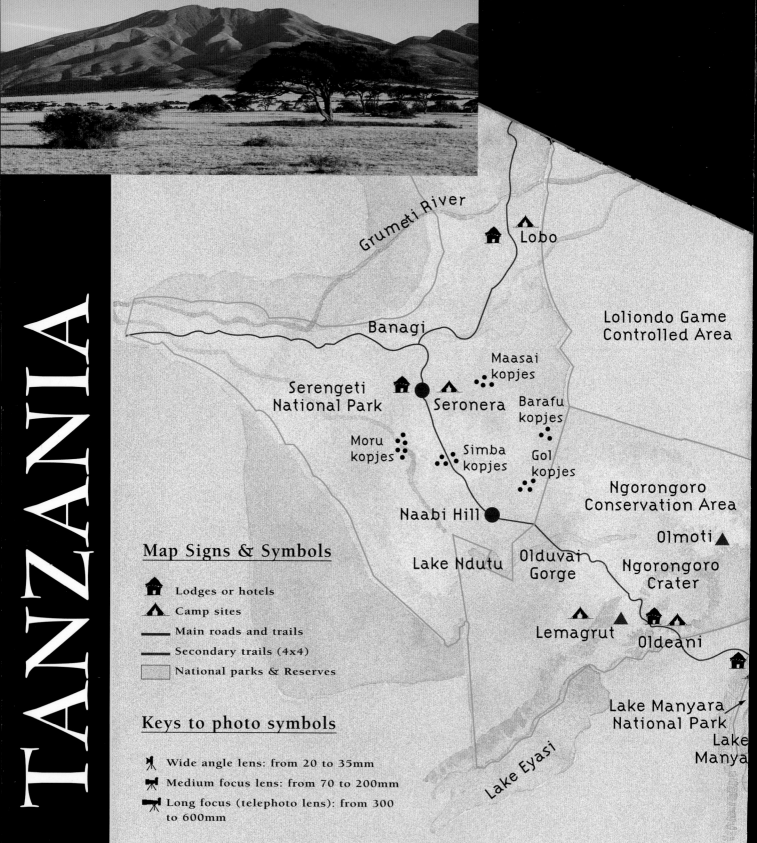

TANZANIA

Map Signs & Symbols

🏠 Lodges or hotels
⛺ Camp sites
▬▬ Main roads and trails
▬▬ Secondary trails (4x4)
▢ National parks & Reserves

Keys to photo symbols

📷 Wide angle lens: from 20 to 35mm
📷 Medium focus lens: from 70 to 200mm
📷 Long focus (telephoto lens): from 300 to 600mm

Grumeti River

Lobo

Loliondo Game Controlled Area

Banagi

Maasai kopjes

Serengeti National Park

Seronera

Barafu kopjes

Moru kopjes

Simba kopjes

Gol kopjes

Ngorongoro Conservation Area

Naabi Hill

Olmoti

Lake Ndutu

Olduvai Gorge

Ngorongoro Crater

Lemagrut

Oldeani

Lake Manyara National Park

Lake Manya

Lake Eyasi

Contents

KENYA

Lake Natron

Ol Doinyo Lengai

npakai

RIFT VALLEY

Mt Kilimanjaro 5896 m

Kilimanjaro National Park

Arusha National Park
Mt Meru

ARUSHA

Tarangire National Park

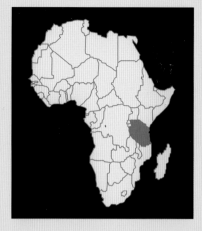

Long overlooked by foreign visitors in favour of adjacent Kenya, Tanzania is none the less the leading refuge for wildlife in the entire African continent. Tourism is still only moderately developed here, not only because of the shortage of accommodation and transport facilities but also the high expense of the National Park entrance fees and residence charges. But this outstandingly beautiful country is still an ideal destination for anyone who wants to discover the wild Africa. It remains largely unchanged by human impact; a land of perpetual light and grandiose scenery, inhabited by legendary animals.

TANZANIA

The state of Tanzania was founded in 1964 after the independence of Tanganyika and Zanzibar, along with the island of Pemba. The total area of its mainland and this island is equivalent to about twice that of France, for a population of just 29 million. The country's borders are more natural than political. Tanzania is like a 'mainland island', bounded on many sides by water. It is separated from Uganda by Lake Victoria, whilst the volcanic range, with its highest points of Mounts Meru and Kilimanjaro, lie on the Kenyan border to the north. The immense Lake Tanganyika forms the boundary to Zaire in the west, and the Mbeya highlands along with Lake Malawi define the limits of Zambia to the south-west. Mozambique lies to the south of Tanzania and shares the Indian Ocean coast, which forms Tanzania's 800-kilometre long eastern boundary.

Described generally as 'tropical temperate', the Tanzanian climate does exhibit some notable local variations. The coastal zone enjoys a warm, damp climate due to the monsoons coming in from the Indian Ocean, while the higher ground has significant rainfall, but escapes the constant high humidity so typical of equatorial regions. The rainy seasons (March to June, then November to December) alternate with the dry seasons. Temperatures vary little, reaching their maximum in December and January, with June and July the coolest months of the year.

Like Kenya, the relief of Tanzania is defined by the Great Rift Valley, with which the geological history of East Africa is inextricably linked. Thirty million years ago, violent upheavals of the Earth's crust

led to a process of fracturing that created a gigantic trough fault — the one that today cuts through the continental plate for around 6,500 kilometres, from Eritrea to Mozambique. Quite apart from its spectacular escarpments, the Rift Valley is distinguished by deep valleys containing numerous lakes. Together, Lakes Natron, Manyara, Eyasi, Kivu, Tanganyika, Rukwa, Malawi and others provide Tanzania with the largest reserves of water within Africa. Tanzania consists primarily of a vast central plateau lying at an altitude varying between 1,000 and 2,000 metres. Higher in the north, towards the south the land slopes downwards to form the coastal plain. The majestic peak of Kilimanjaro, dominating the whole of Africa from its height of 5,896 metres, lies just 250 kilometres from the pale sand beaches. Although

75 percent of the territory is covered by shrub savannah, the mountains, plains and lakes offer a wonderful diversity of habitats supporting the largest concentration of animals on the planet.

Tanzania has such a wealth of wildlife, we had trouble choosing where to focus. We ended up selecting Lake Manyara National Park, its rainforest trapped between the lake and the imposing Rift Valley cliff and the Ngorongoro with its blue-green landscapes. Not far away is Olduvai Gorge, regarded as the cradle of mankind. The Serengeti, the best known of all the Tanzanian parks, has vast plains, millions of herbivores and their predators, arguably the finest spectacle of the bush. To complete this tour we describe Tarangire, with its renowned forest of baobab trees and its exceptional elephant population.

 Lake Manyara lies below the Rift Valley's western escarpment. At the end of the rainy season, the sunrises under the heavy, damp clouds give a different kind of relief to the sky – and to the picture. A wide angle lens is best for capturing the depth of the landscape and the whole palette of twilight colours reflecting in the surface of the lake.

Lake Manyara

S et up in 1960, Lake Manyara National Park occupies around 350 square kilometres, and includes the northern part of the lake itself, which comprises two thirds of the Park. From high up on the side of the Rift Valley there's a stunning panorama stretching out across the Park below. You can make out the bluish silhouette of Mount Meru and the distant Maasai savannahs, as well as the dark green nuances of the forest canopy contrasting with the purple of the lake. This extraordinary abundance of water makes Manyara an unusual part of the country. After a journey through the volcanic subsoils of the high plateaus, many rivers and mountain torrents discharge their pure, crystalline water along the abrupt slopes of the escarpment, feeding the three ecosystems that comprise the territory of the National Park.

The elephants like to take
cover under the trees to
protect themselves from the
sun and to feed. They tend to
move around in families, and
the behaviour of the infants

always makes a touching sight.
To avoid disturbing the group
and risk angering the matriarch,
it is best to use a telephoto to
gain a close up of a young
calf like this.

Manyara's most distinctive habitat is undoubtedly
the rainforest, which would not exist without the
water from the uplands. Some gigantic tropical trees
have developed here. Amongst them thrive the Natal
mahogany, strangler figs, and crotons, whilst wild
mangoes and sausage trees (or kigelias) grow in the
drier zones. This habitat is colonised by a great
many primates, especially baboons, vervet monkeys,
and blue or diademed monkeys. The vegetation can
make it difficult to spot animals that are often
discreet, but the attentive visitor will be able to see
buffalo, waterbuck, bushbuck and, more rarely,
a few elephants and perhaps a leopard. Amongst the
birds, hornbills are very commonly seen, especially
trumpeter and silvery-cheeked hornbills.

Manyara's luxuriant forest shelters
a wealth of fauna, and we set off
on foot via the sometimes steep
footpaths to discover a few animals,
such as these baboons. A hike in
this tropical environment is an
opportunity to use short and
medium focal length lenses to
convey the steamy heat of the
environment. A macro lens can also
be useful for capturing some detail
of the vegetation or for seeking
more abstract compositions.

Alongside the rainforest is a stretch of tree savannah, mainly umbrella acacia and a few baobabs along with thorny scrub. This is the zone where you are most likely to see the tree lions that have done so much for Manyara's reputation. It is not known whether they climb into the branches to spot their prey or to escape the attacks of the tsetse flies, but sprawled out along an acacia branch they make a rather unusual sight. Giraffe, warthog, buffalo, and impala, along with

Normally quite docile, giraffe will happily let you get close to them. A portrait like this one demands a telephoto, lodged firmly on a beanbag. But it takes a great deal more patience to be lucky enough to capture behaviour like this attempted mating. An intimate scene of this sort requires a medium telephoto lens.

Photographing in the raw light of a cloudless early morning gives pictures exceptional colours and contrast. The surface of the water forms a background of fairly even tones, setting off the subjects and in certain cases creating a perfect reflection in the mirror-like water. Needless to say, a telephoto is perfect for shots like this.

other varieties of antelope, are present in this open habitat – also one of the favourite playgrounds of the dwarf mongoose.

The elephant population in this part of the Park was much reduced by poaching, but it is now protected. The birdlife, particularly teeming at the time of the migrations, includes bee-eaters, rollers and cuckoos, as well as a great variety of falcons, eagles and harriers.

The lake shores, marshes, and rivers form Manyara's aquatic world. Maintained by considerable water tables and by water running off the escarpment, the vegetation of the marshy areas is dominated by cattails and papyrus.

A significant proportion of the Park's 300 species of birds live in this habitat, among them Egyptian goose, Eurasian widgeon, cormorants, and several

The lake and its banks have significant concentrations of bird populations. The yellow-billed storks, ibis, flamingos, ducks, and pelicans that nest close by offer a never-ending spectacle. The photographer will have to decide which lens to use according to the number and size of the birds, as well as what effect they are seeking to convey. Medium and long telephotos are generally the most appropriate in this sort of situation.

kinds of stork, including the marabou and the yellow-billed. Birds are also concentrated around the open shores of the lake. Its brackish waters feed thousands of pelicans and pink flamingos that take off in highly spectacular, noisy, clamorous flocks. Hippos are everywhere, especially at the point where the River Simba widens out to form a Hippo Pool.

15

Ngorongoro Crater

The Ngorongoro Conservation Area was created in 1959, in order to protect the site of Olduvai, and above all the superb Ngorongoro volcanic crater, which has been designated a World Heritage Site. This region is also one of the main territories of the Maasai. As a result, it was necessary to reconcile the needs of nature conservation with the centuries-old presence of these herdsmen. They have retained their right of access to the crater, but by nightfall, everyone has to return to their villages on the outer flanks of the volcano.

Like the seven other volcanoes in the range within the Conservation Area, the Ngorongoro was formed in the same period as the Rift Valley. The lava took advantage of the extreme fragility of the Earth's crust to upwell along the fracture, forming as it cooled a series of gigantic volcanic cones, some of which exploded and collapsed. The Ngorongoro is one of these, as defined by its 20 kilometre diameter caldera – probably the largest in the world. Eroded by millions of years of exposure to wind and rain, the ridges surrounding it reach a height of 2,000 metres and plunge 600 metres towards the bottom of the volcano, creating one of the most fascinating landscapes in Tanzania.

For a general view of the Ngorongoro crater you need to pick your spot carefully to avoid unwanted foreground. A veil of mist often envelops this majestic site and, even when it lifts, the sky remains cloudy. Then you have to wait for the light, imprecise, always subtle, soft as cotton wool. With a camera and a wide angle mounted on a tripod all you have to do is press the shutter, and repeat the shot when the light changes quickly.

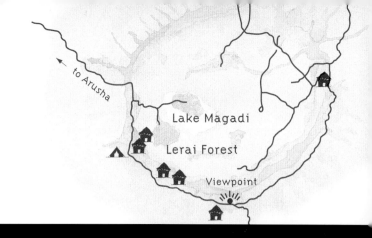

Descending into the crater
involves a long, hard trek, as
the track is steep and rough.
But round every turn in the
path a different, fascinating
spectacle awaits. To convey the
bewitching atmosphere that
envelops this haunting place,
a wide angle or even
panoramic lens is
recommended.

After the rainy season, the savannah turns into a vast field of flowers. This is an opportunity for unusual photos like this long lens shot of buffalo, their gleaming black coats in stark contrast to their floriferous surroundings. Just a few decades ago, this picture would not have been possible because buffalo only started living in the crater around the mid-1970s, when the Maasai and their herds were obliged to leave the area at night-time.

The crater ecosystem is unique. The high rainfall resulting from the equatorial climate provides a permanent water source for both vegetation and animals. On the steep slopes to the east and south, the damp climate sustains an amazing rainforest that is at the heart of the crater's ecological system. It soaks up the water during the rainy season, releasing it again during the dry season as mist, which forms droplets beading the leaves of the trees and shrubs – an invaluable water source for the game. All these factors combined with the geography of the area ensure most of the animals are resident, with only a few moving in and out of the crater.

The exuberant forest that covers the inner slopes of the volcano drapes the landscape in

By nature, the rhinoceros is rather an indolent animal. But when another male threatens his territory, he stirs himself and puts on a show of mock fighting to drive the intruder away. If this intimidation is not enough, the fight becomes real, sometimes resulting in the death of one of the protagonists. The ponderous bodies, the heads carried low, and the swirling dust enveloping the animals — together convey the violence of these clashing titans.

The Ngorongoro crater has become a paradise once again for the black rhinoceros, a few rare individuals of which have set off for the plains in the south of the Serengeti. After years of poaching that have eliminated 80 percent of the population, the species is at last strictly protected and watched over constantly by an army of rangers. One warning: if you go off the tracks or get out of your vehicle to get closer to this rare animal, you will be immediately escorted to the exit of the Conservation Area. Once you have spotted the rhinoceros, it is not difficult to photograph them, though you will want to use a long or medium focus lens to give an impression of the scale of this imposing creature.

bluish-green tints gently filtered by the mist. At the bottom of the crater, a vast savannah punctuated with stands of acacias unrolls its grassy carpet, spiked with thorny bushes. Sun-scorched and dry, or verdant and covered in flowers according to the season, it is visited by the majority of the resident animals. This haven is a refuge for thousands of wildebeest, zebra, and gazelles, hundreds of buffalo, and scores of common eland and waterbuck. Such a concentration of herbivores naturally attracts the predators. Lions, cheetahs, leopards, hyenas, jackals and serval cats find a bountiful larder here. Elephants, particularly males, are rare, doubtless because of their colossal size — if there were more of them, they would soon exhaust the food reserves. The protected black rhinoceros is emblematic of the Ngorongoro — with some twenty individuals here, the crater is the world sanctuary for this severely threatened species.

The early morning mist enveloping the Lerai forest gives the opportunity to photograph a serene atmosphere, while the wildlife is still sluggish with the cool of the night. A medium focus lens made it possible to obtain this fairly general view whilst picking out the monochrome silhouette of the trees.

The crowned cranes are tall wading birds, which offer a magnificent spectacle as they parade and joust. Because they are often a long way from the tracks, it is vital to have a long lens so as not to miss getting a shot.

Watching a mother with her young is always a special moment. Here, the mother lion was suckling its cub. Surprised by our approach, the cub first lifted its head, and then went back to what all youngsters enjoy doing – playing. The attitudes of young are always funny and touching. Even when the light is rather low, it is vital to work fast. You do not get many chances for such an encounter.

It is quite possible to take pictures in low light when it is raining. You need to stay alert and not be afraid to try your luck – the results can sometimes be surprising, as with this lion shaking its soaking mane. A slow shutter speed created the blurring that emphasises the movement and gives the picture a dynamic feel. A long lens was necessary for this unexpected portrait.

An important biotope within the Ngorongoro contains Lake Magadi and the Mandusi and Gorigor marshes. The jade-coloured waters of the alkaline lake are higher during the rainy season. They are home to a profusion of algae, micro-organisms, and fish to satisfy the appetites of numerous aquatic birds like flamingos, ibis, plovers, cormorants, pelicans, herons, and kingfishers. These birds find equally favourable living conditions in the marshy areas too. No less than 250 species of birds have been noted here. Rollers, hornbills, bustards, whydahs, crowned cranes, ostriches, eagles and vultures are amongst the abundant birdlife.

Flamingos large and small colonise the crater's soda lake in their thousands. At random intervals, they take off in a flurry, creating an opportunity for beautiful pictures. A beanbag, or a tripod if you get out of the vehicle, is recommended to ensure a stable camera in variable lighting conditions. The sun breaking through the clouds creates a lovely contrast between the blue slopes of the volcano and the birds in their pink livery.

Olduvai Gorge

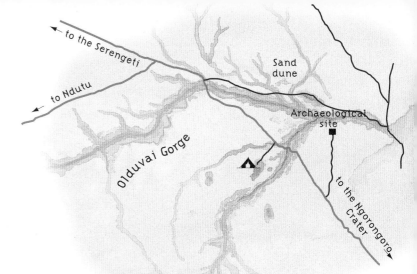

The Ngorongoro Conservation Area is, above all, the land of the Maasai people. You often come across them along the tracks heading down from the crater towards the Olduvai plains. Their tall, slender silhouettes stand out well from the landscape. The green grass and the golden yellow flowers combine with the Maasai's traditional red cloak to offer a beautiful colour composition here. These adolescents allowed themselves to be photographed in exchange for a few shillings. However, it is highly frowned upon to photograph the Maasai against their wishes or surreptitiously.

Located within the territory of the Ngorongoro Conservation Area, the Olduvai Gorge is a crack in the Earth's crust stretching over forty or so kilometres from east to west, along the Serengeti plains. Before it came to be regarded as the cradle of mankind, Olduvai was first and foremost a site of geological interest. In ancient times, a basalt plain was present where the gorge is now. Tectonic activity in the region led to the creation of a lake, which was gradually silted up by the alluvial deposits from fresh volcanic eruptions. The disappearance of the lake left a river and its erosive action created the gorge we know today.

At that time, two species of hominids had already been here, one Australopithecus boisei, the other Homo habilis. The former gradually died out in favour of the latter, which became Homo erectus, capable of hunting and making tools, and then Homo sapiens followed. A million years ago, the climate became abnormally hot and dry, driving man and animals from the region. It would be over 200,000 years before they came back again. The presence of these earliest populations meant Olduvai became a major centre for palaeontological excavations from the early twentieth century

A view taken with a wide angle will give the best idea of what the gorge is really like, from its formation down through the ages of the Earth, shaped by the work of both wind and water. A mineral cradle laden with all the history of mankind, the richness of its fossil-bearing strata makes us dream of the treasures of our origins that they perhaps still hide. But for how much longer? Should the Horn of Africa break away from the continent, the sea would engulf Olduvai.

onwards. But it was not until the late 1950's that Louis and Mary Leakey discovered the remains of Australopithecus boisei. The research by these two anthropologists made it possible to retrace the history of human life over almost two million years. Their discoveries tend to confirm the theory that man originated in Africa. The majority of the oldest human and pre-human fossils have been located in the east of the Great Rift Valley.

Out of all the species of birds in the gorge, the red-and-yellow barbet is commonly seen, often atop a termite mound where it makes a nest, or on an acacia branch not far away. If you can manage to creep upon it, you may even be able to shoot it with a medium focus lens.

A lone giraffe nonchalantly ambles across the plain in front of a volcano backdrop. Before the sun disappears below the horizon its warm light gilds the short grass. Everything is perfect for composing a picture depicting an animal within its environment, using a medium focus lens.

Nowadays, excavations have stopped and the sand and stone labyrinths of the arid, ochre slopes of the gorge are home to a few species of herbivores. Amongst them are small groups of giraffe, eland, and zebra. More rarely, the discreet leopard sometimes makes its lair in the rocky hideaways of the walls. Coming to Olduvai between the months of December and March can be particularly interesting, as the migrating wildebeest stop off here before heading north.

It is always an exceptional stroke of luck to come across a big cat with her young. But take care, the cubs are vulnerable, and disturbing them or distracting their mother's vigilance could be fatal for them.

Even though cheetahs are relatively unafraid, you must keep a reasonable distance away and use a long lens to photograph the striking faces and the antics of the smallest babies.

to Lobo

Seronera

Mbalageti River

Maasai kopjes to Barafu kopjes

Seronera River

The great wildebeest migration is a major event in the animal kingdom and an opportunity to use your whole range of lenses to photograph the multitude of antelopes on the march. Clustering together in columns of thousands of individuals, they head from south to north in search of grazing. The wide angle used for this picture makes it possible to convey the immensity of the herd and also the landscape.

The Serengeti

Set up by the British colonial administration in 1951, the Serengeti is Tanzania's oldest National Park and comprising 14,760 square kilometres, is also the largest. It covers a high plateau where the altitude is between 1,000 and 2,000 metres. It adjoins the Ngorongoro Conservation Area to the south-east, the Maswa Game Reserve to the south-west, and to the north Kenya's Masai Mara reserve, with which it shares the same ecosystem.

Famous first and foremost for its immense plains and its fantastic antelope migrations, the Serengeti contains a great diversity of habitats that are home to the largest concentration of fauna in the whole African continent. It may be divided into several geographic sectors, each comprising different habitats: the south-east with its grassy savannahs dotted with granite outcrops; the central Seronera zone, with its permanent river and open woodland; the north, with the rolling, tree-covered savannahs of the Lobo region; and lastly the western plains and hills where the rivers Grumeti and Mbagaleti wind across the Western Corridor territories.

When you enter the Serengeti from the south, the first sight you see is what you expect – treeless plains stretching away to an infinite horizon devoid of relief. But often, round a bend in the track, the distant,

Where the geography of the terrain allows it, it is helpful to gain some height so as to get a more original angle for your shot. A medium focus lens lets you get more detail of the animals by cropping the frame. The absence of any sky helps convey the concentration and crowding of the wildebeest over the whole length of their slow and inexorable quest for fresh grazing. In the Seronera region, during the months of May and June, hundreds of thousands of them invade the plains as far as the eye can see.

The granite outcrops that break up the horizon of the Serengeti plains appear as islands in a sea of grass. Kopjes range in size, isolation and plant cover and therefore offer an infinite variety of landscapes. Use different lenses to allow for variation in picture composition.

In the language of the Maasai, Serengeti means 'big space' – an apt name for these infinite territories. But all the same it is surprising to note how the scenery and biotopes vary within just a few kilometres of each other, as is shown by this pair of images taken with a medium focus lens.

shadowy blue silhouettes of the volcanic range stand out against the eternally cloudy sky. From November to May, more than two million wildebeest invade these immense spaces. At the first signs of the dry season, around May/June, most of them set off on a 200-kilometre journey northwards to reach the more verdant grazing of the Masai Mara in Kenya, whilst others take the Western Corridor to reach Lake Victoria, and lastly a small group heads for the Ngorongoro. Then come September, they return to graze again in the Serengeti. Thousands of zebra and gazelles follow the laborious, nodding columns of wildebeest. During the first three months of the year, all these animals bear their young. A windfall for the resident predators, who every day feast from the passing herds.

Baby Thomson's gazelles are easy game for the swift cheetahs. Lions will not hesitate to approach without cover to hunt down a young wildebeest or zebra,

On the kopjes, when lions are not lying in the shade of a tree, they may select a promontory to survey the surrounding plains. A telephoto was used for this simple composition. Its clear, graphic structure, heightened by three distinct groups of colours, would have been spoilt by any other intruding element.

39

though they may have to relinquish it to
a pack of ravenous hyenas. Motionless kori
bustards watch the spectacle from afar, while
the secretary birds forage in the grass for
a reptile or small rodent.

Dotted here and there across these arid
savannahs rise granite inselbergs. Known as
kopjes, these eroded rock masses of volcanic
origin come in a wide range of sizes. They
form islands of relatively dense vegetation,
sustained by the rain trapped in the nooks
and crannies.

Within the kopjes grow candelabra euphorbia,
acacias and sausage trees as well as sisals and
aloes. The main kopjes are called Moru, Gol,
Barafu, Simba, and Maasai, and are located

The Serengeti is undoubtedly the
realm of the lions, with what is
indisputably one of the highest
concentrations in Africa. It is quite
common to encounter groups of
several tens of individuals, especially
lionesses with young. The plain
colouring of their coat sometimes
hides them from view. It takes skill
to spot them, as well as very quick
reactions to capture the pose of
a curious lioness raising her head
before disappearing once again
within the long grass.

There are lots of big cats in the Serengeti – some more discreet than others. Cheetahs are the easiest to observe, while servals and leopards are invisible most of the time. A long lens will be your best companion for immortalising these encounters. Photographing these big cats right in the middle of a flower-rich savannah is a photographer's dream that few manage to make come true. But the location is so exceptional, and the pictures produced so diametrically opposed to what you usually see of Africa, you could hardly fail to appreciate them.

principally in the south-east of the Park. Their random configuration offers plenty of hiding places for animals. Hyrax and mongooses have settled here, side by side with the countless red-headed rock agama lizards that can often be seen sunbathing motionless on a flat rock. Although present, the spitting cobra and puff adder are seen much less often. Birds of prey, such as the black eagle, nest in hidden corners. The jackal, serval and caracal also choose to live amongst this maze of rocks, where you will sometimes see a lion or even a leopard lounging in the shade of a sausage tree.

Right in the heart of the cheetahs' hunting country, the kopjes are a cool haven. Here they seek out welcome shade, when metallic rays of the sun beat down on the rock turning it to glistening steel.

Lions are not always the bloodthirsty killers that we tell children about. Spending several hours with them gives you the opportunity to see that they can have tender gestures, even between adults. Here again, a long lens ensures an optimal result.

The quizzical pose of these young lion cubs is arresting. They seem to be intrigued, all their attention is focused, their senses alert. The low-angle front lighting perfectly picks out their faces and paints the picture in a gentle warmth. The telephoto is ideal, but take care with the angle of the shot. The animals are small, so it is preferable to photograph them from a window, rather than through the roof of the vehicle, to avoid too high an angle shot looking down on them.

At the geographic centre of the Serengeti, the Seronera region probably attracts the greatest number of animals in the whole Park. Its open brush woodlands are composed of trees with a graphic, geometric quality that makes for photogenic scenes. On the topmost branches of the yellow fever tree, it's not unusual to see several bateleur eagles, and occasionally vultures or other equally impressive birds of prey.

In the undergrowth, a soft light catches the russet fur of the hartebeest, to the sound of the baboons' piercing cries. Topi, waterbuck, dik-dik, and Defassa waterbuck, as well as the discreet reedbuck, also like this open woodland space where they can find food in abundance. In the shade of the umbrella acacia clumps, elephants crop the shoots of nourishing

Following a trail on the savannah means always being on the path to discovery. Here, (below) a herd of impala are sharing the lush grass with zebra. There, (left) some wildebeest pause to drink. Further off, elephants head for a clump of trees, nibbling a few tender grass shoots in passing. Medium focus and long lenses make this type of shot possible, as when the animals are active, it is better not to disturb them by getting too close. Occasionally they may take the initiative to move in closer.

grass, leaving the youngest to wrestle in the dust. Often too, lions laze under the benevolent cover of the trees. Herons, yellow-billed storks, egrets, and saddle-billed storks visit the river; all going about their business beneath the indifferent gaze of the hippos immersed in the brackish water.

At drinking time, the zebra and wildebeest approach the banks of the river cautiously; some of them take advantage of it to bathe. But the slightest suspicious movement and they all bolt amidst sprays of brown water. Along the banks of the river stands a gallery forest, where, if you are patient and watchful, you are quite likely to discover the presence of a solitary leopard, reclining on a branch.

This photo is especially interesting because of the lion's pose. Only its head and paw are visible between the rocks, as if it had become a big pussycat again and hidden, the better to spy on possible prey — unless he was afraid of some danger. You cannot help smiling at this gentle pose of the most powerful predator on the savannah.

Most of the animals in the Serengeti take advantage of the kopjes dotted around. The lions, in particular, find water to drink and trees to protect them from the heat. But when the temperature is more comfortable, they do enjoy lounging on a sun-warmed rock. For the youngest, this is a new playground. This picture needed a telephoto, whereas a zoom or medium focus lens allows for variation in framing the assemblage of plants and rocks within each kopje. Here again, the plain sky strengthens the tonal contrasts of the landscape.

Lowering clouds and a dark curtain of rain blanket the horizon – but the leopard was there. So was a graphic picture too. The cat's silhouette stands out clearly against the stormy sky. A medium focus lens, held very steady because of the low light, made it possible to capture this ephemeral composition.

On safari, searching for a leopard demands a keen eye and a dogged determination. The animal likes trees, where it is in the habit of stashing its prey, to protect it from the carrion-eating competition. When its dappled coat blends into the surroundings, you need to carefully scrutinise the foliage, the forks and boughs - even the highest ones.

North of Seronera, the Banagi and Lobo regions are characterised by undulating relief covered with brush savannah, scattered clumps of woodland, dotted in places with kopjes. The wildebeest are obliged to pass through here during their seasonal migration, as they come and go between the Masai Mara and the southern plains.

Thousands of zebra and gazelles accompany them in the dust, the sunlight beating down on their slowly advancing columns. Numerous predators take advantage of this providential manna. Watching a fight between giraffes, lions mating, and an impala giving birth, are just a few of the many spectacles of the bush. By the same token, the significant

numbers of buffalos, cheetahs, and ostriches in particular, offer the prospect of some captivating sights. Although less rare, the serval does make the odd appearance from time to time. Around Lobo there is also a population of around 800 elephants. Moreover, the Grumeti, Bologonja and Mara rivers that cross the region are permanent sources of water that encourage animals to gather, especially in the dry season. All year round the wild fig trees and mahoganies of the adjoining forests shelter a wealth of birdlife. Touracos, kingfishers and fish-eagles are amongst the numerous species populating this Garden of Eden.

The Western Corridor sector too, is famous for being one of the preferred routes for the great wildebeest migration. Clearly delimited by the rivers Grumeti and Mbagaleti, the Corridor is a mosaic of rolling hills and plains of black clay, which turn into a sticky mire that is best avoided in the rainy season. Funnelled by the topography, thousands of snorting, grunting antelope advance laboriously towards the northern pastures. To reach them, they have to cross the River Grumeti.

The low-angled rays of the sun at sunset model the texture of the elephants' thick hide. The intense colours give these two pictures, taken a few minutes apart from the same spot, a very beautiful atmosphere. The light appears different because we had to follow the animals' progress without moving our vehicle. They came towards us in single file, and then went round us to reach the river further on. Their close approach made it possible to use a medium focus lens. But the fading light meant the camera had to be perfectly steady. Cropping the pictures to a panoramic format concentrates the interest, making them more powerful and more original.

The smallest bird of prey on the entire continent, the pygmy falcon frequently perches on a bare branch to survey its hunting grounds. Even when fairly close to this miniature falcon, a very long lens is necessary. Here the light filtering through the foliage, the bird's greyish plumage, and its gleaming eye give the picture a beautiful feel.

Capturing a bird of prey in flight is a difficult exercise, but there is always plenty of opportunity to have a go. A long lens is highly recommended, but without a monopod it requires strength to hold it at arm's length.

Getting this close to a secretary bird is exceptional. This 'long-legged bird of prey' is very shy and a telephoto is always required. It frequents the great wide-open spaces of the plains and usually lives in pairs.

This would be no real obstacle with only a few animals, but in reality the crossings are doubly dangerous. Many wildebeest will die, drowned or trampled by their fellows or snatched by the voracious Nile crocodiles. The Kirawira site has the greatest concentration of these enormous reptiles, some over five metres long. Even apart from the migration, the Western Corridor is a vast animal reservoir. The forests lining the banks of the Grumeti shelter the rare eastern black-and-white colobus monkey, elegant in its long, bi-coloured fur.

Here, under cover of the vegetation a leopard waits to prey on an unsuspecting monkey. Also present, although more discreet and often with nocturnal habits, are civets, genets, caracals, bat-eared foxes, oribis, duikers, pangolins and aardwolves.

There are often warm tones along the rivers. The gallery forests delicately filter the sunlight and the colours of the foliage are heightened in the surface of the brackish water. Landscape enthusiasts will use wide angle or medium lenses in particular.

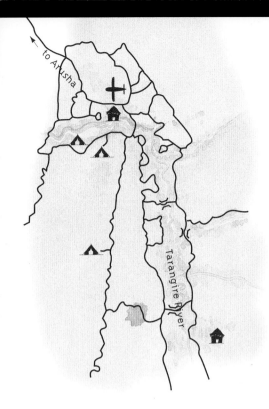

Tarangire

The large number of tsetse flies makes Tarangire unsuitable for agriculture and livestock farming. This is one of the reasons for its present status. Originally a game reserve, then from 1970 a National Park, Tarangire consists of a plateau and undulating plains crossed by the eponymous river that empties into Lake Burungi to the north. At an altitude of over 1,000 metres, a jigsaw puzzle of forests, hills, marshes and dry savannahs covers the 2,600 square kilometres of the park.

The northern part consists of a wooded savannah with baobab trees over a hundred years old. Their monumental silhouette is the most striking characteristic of the Park's scenery; their scored trunks bear witness to the many elephants who come to pillage the water reserves stored in them. Having at one time been the victims of intensive poaching, the elephants that created the Park's reputation are at last protected and their population is now some 3,000 individuals.

As elsewhere in Africa, the sunsets in Tanzania are magnificent. Sometimes there is no more than a glow of light to give the photo an air of mystery. Photographing the sunset is a simple pleasure you should not forgo. Depending on how you want to crop the frame, all lenses may be used. Here, a medium lens was chosen to bring out the detail of Tarangire's typical baobab forest.

There is a considerable population of black kites in Africa, their presence almost always associated with human activity. When picnicking in the bush, you need to take care, as this thieving bird of prey does not hesitate to make a dive for a sandwich, even if you are holding it in your hand. The power of its sharp talons and its speed in action make it a dangerous animal. The bird is no less fine for all that, and can be photographed in flight, when it is not paying attention. To pull off a shot like this, you need to use a telephoto lens and set the camera to shutter priority.

In the dry season, the smallest pond becomes a gathering-place for a multitude of birds. It is a place worth hanging around for a few shots – with a telephoto, of course! It is a rare sight to find a group of blacksmith plover like this, as it is a monogamous, territorial bird generally found in pairs.

Further to the east, clumps of acacias and scrubby bush alternate to create a habitat that encourages major gatherings of herbivores. Giraffe, eland, wildebeest, impala, waterbuck, and kudu find significant food reserves here. Baboons and vervet monkeys are not uncommon. You can sometimes spot a family of banded mongooses scurrying off to their burrows, beneath the surprised gaze of a southern ground hornbill.

When the sun fades behind leaden rain-bearing clouds, frequent inundations of the plains create seasonal marshes. A vast marshy zone stretching southwards then occupies the centre of the Park. A considerable variety of birdlife occurs here. The birds of prey are majestically represented by all kinds of eagles and vultures, with hammerkops, saddle-billed, yellow-billed and marabou storks to complete the list. Lots of reedbuck and hippos also come here. The acacias next to these wetlands are noted for sheltering pythons – not always easy to spot as they secretly nestle in the vegetation.

Distinguished by both the colouration and its rolling flight, the bateleur eagle is abundant in this area. Although these birds of prey spend more than eight hours a day gliding in the air, spotting an individual motionless on a branch is not unusual. A long lens is indispensable to take such a portrait of this spectacular bird of prey.

Young male elephants often engage in jousting matches for training. Closer to play than fighting, they foreshadow the genuine confrontations they will have to face when they are adult, notably as rival males, contesting to win a female. But perhaps we have just been watching one of the tactile recognitions that help bind elephant social ties so solidly. That morning, in the clear light and thanks to long and medium focus lenses, we were able to photograph this behaviour repeatedly.

Tarangire has a major giraffe population, and it is quite common to see them in large groups. Here a female seemed to be watching over her own young and that of her fellows. The impossibility of getting close to the animals has naturally favoured the use of the telephoto. The presence of the giraffe calves generates the main interest in this photo, which is also interesting for the clarity of the light that enhances the details of the image.

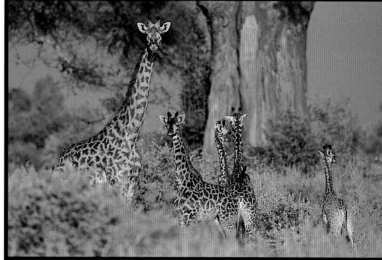

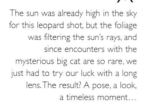

The sun was already high in the sky for this leopard shot, but the foliage was filtering the sun's rays, and since encounters with the mysterious big cat are so rare, we just had to try our luck with a long lens. The result? A pose, a look, a timeless moment…

The south of Tarangire is a collection of wooded hills, grassy savannahs, and waterholes, although the only permanent source of water is the river that winds through the Park. Animals congregate around it, especially in the dry season, upon their return from the exodus that dispersed them over several thousands of square kilometres. Buffalo, Grant's and Thomson's gazelles, topi and zebra come to join the resident species such as giraffe, dik-dik, and lesser kudu. The rare gerenuk is occasionally seen here too, although it is at the extreme limit of its distribution area within the Park.

After rain, the air is purified. It lets through the rays of the evening sunlight that reveal the relief of the river cliffs and outline the sparse foliage of the trees on the ridge. The anthracite grey sky provides powerful contrast, contributing greatly to the picture's depth. A wide angle was perfect to embrace this mosaic of light and colours.

Informations pratiques

FORMALITIES
Visa.

HEALTH
Yellow fever vaccination obligatory (wherever possible, carry your vaccination certificate). Anti-malarial treatment advisable.

LANGUAGE
Swahili and English.

CURRENCY
Tanzanian shilling.

ELECTRICITY
230 volts; round pins and regular blade plugs.

TIME ZONE
GMT + 3 hours.

WEATHER
Rather hot, with a small temperature variation from one season to another. Temperatures comfortable all year round. Watch out for coolness at higher altitudes. Rains in November/December and from March to June.

LUGGAGE
Clothing: light for daytime: shirts, T-shirts, trousers, Bermuda shorts, shorts; warm for morning and evening: pullover, fleece (especially for the Crater), lightweight jacket. Shoes: one pair of stout, high-topped walking shoes and a light pair. Other: hat, sunglasses, sunscreen, anti-mosquito lotion, torch, personal pharmacy, passport with visa, plane ticket, credit card and local currency in cash.

PHOTO EQUIPMENT
Camera bodies, lenses, flash, filters, films, spare batteries, rechargeable batteries (do bear in mind that digital equipment is very power-thirsty), cleaning kit (blower, brush, soft cloth), beanbag (excellent stabiliser for vehicle windows), bag to protect against dust. Be sure to carry film in your carry-on baggage because the powerful x-rays used on checked baggage will harm films. Photographers using digital equipment should take plenty of memory cards as well as a portable hard drive to offload their image files and free memory cards prior to processing files upon returning home. Two camera bodies will reduce the risk of getting dust on the sensor caused by repeatedly changing lenses.

ACCOMMODATION
There is sufficient variety of accommodation for you to be able to choose what is most suitable for your trip. For our various stays in Tanzania, we have tried out certain lodges, bush camps, and fixed camps. Naturally, our preference is for the bush camps. These are tents with communal facilities, pitched upon request within the Parks, where you choose the location from the list provided by the authorities. The camping sites are always in the heart of the bush, facing the rising sun. The animals come and go in complete freedom all round. Sleep is punctuated by the lions' throaty growls and the cries of the hyena. Less rudimentary than a bivouac, this type of

accommodation guarantees excitement. The lodges are comfortable, but despite being built as close as possible to the centres of interest, the infrastructure they require keeps animal activity at a distance. So it is up to you to make the choice between comfort and excitement.

GETTING AROUND

You can get around in a minibus or a 4x4. Here again, everything depends on the route. Naturally, 4x4 vehicles allow greater freedom on terrain that is not always accessible. They generally have sliding windows, so it is possible to fit a shelf that will support long lenses when used with a beanbag. Vehicles with a sunroof are very convenient for shooting down from a high angle.

PARKS AND RESERVES

The National Parks in Tanzania are entirely and exclusively devoted to the protection of nature and tourism. The country has

fourteen parks: the Serengeti, Ruaha, Mikumi, Tarangire, Katavi, Mahale Mountains, Udzungwa, Kilimanjaro, Manyara, Rubondo Island, Arusha, Gombe Stream, Kitulo Plateau and Saadani. The Ngorongoro has a special status. Designated a World Heritage Site, within the Conservation Area, nature is strictly protected, but the Maasai are allowed to water their herds between sunrise and sunset. The 'game reserves' on the other hand are private territories where regulated hunting is tolerated and sometimes even organised. But the landowners usually devote one part of their land to fauna conservation, and welcome photo safaris. Selous is a typical example. Together, the Parks and Reserves in Tanzania represent over 20 percent of the territory. In 1989, Lake Manyara, the Serengeti National Park and the Ngorongoro Crater were added to the list of world Biosphere Reserves.

Wildlife Photography

Whether you are an amateur or a professional nature photographer you need to be very familiar with the wildlife. So you need to find out all you can about your destination. The season: what's the climate like? What's the light like? The period: the mating season? The migration season? How many films or memory cards to take so as not to miss anything of the animals' intense activity? The region: what sort of vegetation? What sort of relief? Will you need flash? The terrain: what sort of tracks? How long does it take to get from one site to another? The fauna: what species? What concentrations? What focal length lens to choose? Knowledge of this information, and a lot more besides, contributes generally to a successful stay. But when wildlife photographers are heading far afield, they tend to take everything with them; ultimately, they are right to do so! The scenery and vegetation of the sites visited are often so rich, and the animals offer such unexpected behaviour, that it is wise to have all your lenses available to cover every situation.

Very long 400, 500 or 600mm lenses are ideal for animal portraits, or even capturing the detail of their gaze. But if you cannot get hold of this type of lens, a 300mm with a tele-converter can do the job quite well. A medium focus lens, such as 200mm make it possible to place animals in their context, or to capture a scene with several individuals. To convey the immensity of the landscapes, and of the sky too, to maintain the depth of the elements and their infinite palette of colours, a wide angle zoom is irreplaceable. But you must never forget speed, too, forms part of the photographer's talent, which is why several bodies are indispensable, to avoid untimely lens changing while an action is going on.

In terms of photography, safaris are not the easiest discipline. Being obliged to always stay inside the vehicle and never straying off the tracks are very restricting factors that sometimes seem to limit the possibility for choosing the angles for your shots. But the safari companies do offer the public, vehicles that are ideally suited with highly competent drivers, to allow the greatest freedom of movement. Knowing if you will have a window, a sunroof, or both allows you to plan your accessories. The completely open 4x4s common in southern Africa are less widespread in east Africa, so a monopod will not be essential. But on the other hand, a beanbag is vital. Long lenses need to be steadied in some way. A bag three-quarters filled with rice, dried beans or peas ensures this stability by moulding itself

to the shape of the camera. The resulting increased steadiness means it becomes possible to shoot in low-light conditions with quite slow shutter speeds. Photographing nature also means having exceptional patience, for you can never really know the animal, even though you may occasionally be able to anticipate its behaviour. You need to know how long to wait. Waiting several minutes or several hours before the cheetah gets up to go hunting, before the hippopotamus attacks its fellow, before the gazelle gives birth, before the fish eagle whisks a fish up into the air. Simply waiting for the sun to reappear from behind the clouds to illuminate the flower-covered savannah after a storm. Seeking to document, as well as to create. Seeking out new angles, new lights, a new graphic quality. Making use of the basic rules of photography, embracing them so as to bend them better. Do not worry if you miss a picture, there will be other chances. But first, you need to take time. Look, spot, observe, listen, understand, and be curious all the time.

Photographing nature is a whole discipline in itself, always with fresh interest because of the conditions on the ground, which are different every time. But what makes the quality of a picture above all else is the photographer's curiosity and creativity. Experience should allow photographers to be constantly re-appraising and challenging their own work and to progress still further – to better surprise, to better astound, to better make the viewer dream.